# Tomato

## A tantalizing tour of ravishing recipes

Judy Williams

p

This is a Parragon Publishing Book
First published in 2004

Parragon Publishing
Queen Street House
4 Queen Street
Bath
BA1 1HE
United Kingdom



ISBN: 1-40542-955-0

Printed in Indonesia

Produced by the BRIDGEWATER BOOK COMPANY LTD

Photographer: Karen Thomas
Prop Stylist: Karen Thomas
Food Stylist: Justine Pattison

**Note**
This book uses imperial, metric, or US cup measurements. Follow the same units of measurement throughout; do not mix imperial and metric. All spoon measurements are level: teaspoons are assumed to be 5 ml, and tablespoons are assumed to be 15 ml. Unless otherwise stated, milk is assumed to be whole, eggs and individual vegetables such as potatoes are medium, and pepper is freshly ground black pepper.

The times given are an approximate guide only. The preparation times may differ according to the techniques used by different people and the cooking times may vary as a result of the type of oven used.

Recipes using raw or very lightly cooked eggs should be avoided by infants, the elderly, pregnant women, convalescents, and anyone suffering from an illness. Pregnant and breastfeeding women are advised to avoid eating peanuts and peanut products.

# Contents

# Introduction

AVAILABLE ALL YEAR *round and in a delicious range of shapes and sizes, the tomato must be one of the most popular and useful foods in the world. Its versatile flavor, shape, and texture enable the tomato to be used in many different ways, from a raw addition to salads and salsas to a pulped essential for sauces, curries, and pastes. The tomato is thought to have originated in South America, probably Peru, although this was a very different fruit from the modern variety. Long stems held tiny fruits that were only edible when they turned red and usually split open while still on the plant. Eventually, the tomato was transported round the world and began its transformation into the wonderful fruit we know today.*

*There was a time when people were very suspicious of the tomato, thinking it had special properties because of its links to the potato and deadly nightshade family. This in turn led to the belief that tomatoes acted as an aphrodisiac. Even today, recipes using tomatoes are often published around Valentine's Day.*

*Most of us have grown our own tomatoes, as they are easily cultivated and there is nothing like picking ripe tomatoes straight from the plant. The distinctive smell of the tomato actually comes from the stem. This seductive scent, along with the vibrant color, makes the tomato an ingredient of unique distinction.*

# Tomato & Mango Salsa

**SERVES 4–6**

PREPARATION TIME: 10 MINUTES

COOKING TIME: 5–10 MINUTES

6 medium ripe tomatoes
1 tbsp oil
1 onion, finely chopped
1 large mango, halved, seeded, peeled, and diced
2 tbsp chopped fresh cilantro
salt and pepper
tortilla chips, to serve

*Choose tomatoes that are soft to the touch for a sweet taste. This salsa is delicious spooned over poached fish.*

**1** Place the tomatoes in a large bowl. Cover with boiling water and let stand for 1 minute, then lift out. Using a knife, pierce the skin and peel it off. Cut the tomato into quarters, then cut out the central core and seeds. Chop the remaining flesh and place in a large bowl.

**2** Heat the oil in a skillet. Add the onion and gently cook until softened. Add to the bowl of tomatoes together with the mango and cilantro. Season to taste with salt and pepper.

**3** Serve cold with tortilla chips.

# Speedy Tomato Relish

**SERVES 6–8**

PREPARATION TIME: 10 MINUTES, PLUS 30 MINUTES COOLING

COOKING TIME: 15 MINUTES

2 large cooking apples, peeled, quartered, cored, and chopped
2 tbsp superfine sugar
1/2 tsp ground allspice
4–5 cloves
2 tbsp water
1 tbsp oil
1 large red onion, coarsely chopped
6 tomatoes, peeled and chopped (see page 6)

*Toss the peeled apples in a little lemon juice to prevent them going brown. Serve with sausages or pork chops.*

**1** Place the apples, sugar, allspice, and cloves in a large pan. Add the water and cook gently until softened but not puréed.

**2** Heat the oil in a large skillet. Add the onion and cook until softened. Add the tomatoes and stir together for 30 seconds. Add to the apples, mix well, and let the mixture cool.

**3** Transfer the relish to a clean jar, cover, and store in the refrigerator for 3–4 days.

# Tomato Sauce

**SERVES 2**

PREPARATION TIME: 10 MINUTES

COOKING TIME: 25 MINUTES

1 tbsp oil

1 onion, finely chopped

1 garlic clove, finely chopped

6 tomatoes, peeled, seeded, and chopped (see page 6)

1 oz/25 g anchovies, coarsely chopped

6 black olives, pitted and coarsely chopped

2 tbsp fresh basil leaves, coarsely shredded

salt and pepper

*Use dry black olives for extra flavor. This sauce is delicious stirred through pasta and topped with grated Parmesan cheese.*

**1** Heat the oil in a large skillet. Add the onion and garlic and cook over low heat for 10 minutes, until very soft. Add the tomatoes and cook for an additional 10–12 minutes, until the mixture is pulpy.

**2** Add the anchovies, olives, basil leaves, and salt and pepper to taste and cook gently until all the ingredients are hot.

**3** Serve at once.

# Gazpacho

*This soup is best served very cold and eaten on hot, sunny days.*

**1** Set aside some of the tomatoes, cucumber, and bell pepper for a garnish. Place the bread into a food processor and process until crumbs form. Add the remaining tomatoes, cucumber, and bell pepper. Add the onion, garlic, vinegar, and oil and process until smooth.

**2** The tomatoes should have enough juice in them to make enough liquid but add a little water if the soup is too thick. Season to taste with salt.

**3** Divide the soup between 4 serving bowls and add a few ice cubes to make sure that the soup is served chilled. Garnish with the reserved tomatoes, cucumber, and bell pepper. Add a few sprigs of basil and serve with fresh crusty bread.

**SERVES 4**

PREPARATION TIME: 20 MINUTES

COOKING TIME: NONE

2 lb 4 oz/1 kg ripe tomatoes, peeled, seeded, and coarsely chopped (see page 6)

1/2 cucumber, peeled, seeded, and coarsely chopped

1 green bell pepper, seeded and coarsely chopped

4 oz/115 g fresh bread, crusts removed

1 small onion, coarsely chopped

1 garlic clove, chopped

1 tbsp white wine vinegar

1/2 cup medium olive oil

salt to taste

ice cubes

few fresh basil sprigs, to garnish

fresh crusty bread, to serve

# Tomato & Red Onion Relish

**SERVES 4**

PREPARATION TIME: 15 MINUTES

COOKING TIME: 1 HOUR 25 MINUTES–
1 HOUR 40 MINUTES

**For the oven-dried tomatoes**

8 ripe tomatoes

1–2 tbsp virgin olive oil

salt and pepper

**For the sauce**

1 tbsp virgin olive oil

2 large red onions, thinly sliced

1 1/4 cups arugula or baby spinach leaves

*These tomatoes have a stronger flavor than fresh ones. Serve as an accompaniment to sausages, chicken, or fish, or with a jacket potato for a tasty lunch or snack.*

**1** For the oven-dried tomatoes, preheat the oven to 300°F/ 150°C. Cut the tomatoes in half, cut out the cores, and arrange all the halves in a large roasting pan. Drizzle with the oil and season well with salt and pepper. Cook in the oven for 1 1/4–1 1/2 hours, or until roasted but still moist.

**2** For the sauce, heat the oil in a large skillet. Add the onions and cook over gentle heat until soft and golden brown. Place 8 of the oven-dried tomatoes in a food processor and process until puréed. Add to the onions in the skillet.

**3** Slice the remaining 8 tomato halves and add to the skillet with the arugula. Season to taste with salt and pepper and cook until the leaves have just wilted. Serve at once.

# Tomato, Mozzarella & Avocado Salad

**SERVES 4**

PREPARATION TIME: 15 MINUTES

COOKING TIME: NONE

2 ripe beefsteak tomatoes
5 1/2 oz/150 g fresh mozzarella cheese
2 avocados
4 tbsp olive oil
1 1/2 tbsp white wine vinegar
1 tsp coarse grain mustard
salt and pepper
few fresh basil leaves, torn into pieces
20 black olives
fresh crusty bread, to serve

*This is a familiar and popular salad that makes a wonderful lunch with fresh bread.*

**1** Using a sharp knife, cut the tomatoes into thick wedges and place in a large serving dish. Drain the mozzarella cheese and coarsely tear into pieces. Cut the avocados in half and remove the pits. Cut the flesh into slices, then arrange the mozzarella cheese and avocado with the tomatoes.

**2** Mix the oil, vinegar, and mustard together in a small bowl, add salt and pepper to taste, then drizzle over the salad.

**3** Sprinkle the basil and olives over the top and serve at once with fresh crusty bread.

# Tomato, Salmon & Shrimp Salad

*Mixing different types of tomatoes together adds extra flavor to this salad. Add some of the sungold ones if available.*

**1** Halve most of the cherry tomatoes. Place the lettuce leaves round the edge of a shallow bowl and add all the tomatoes and cherry tomatoes. Using scissors, snip the smoked salmon into strips and sprinkle over the tomatoes, then add the shrimp.

**2** Mix the mustard, sugar, vinegar, and oil together in a small bowl, then tear most of the dill sprigs into it. Mix well and pour over the salad. Toss well to coat the salad with the dressing. Snip the remaining dill over the top and season to taste with pepper.

**3** Serve the salad with warmed rolls or ciabatta bread.

**SERVES 4**

PREPARATION TIME: 20 MINUTES

COOKING TIME: NONE

4 oz/115 g cherry or baby plum tomatoes

several lettuce leaves

4 ripe tomatoes, coarsely chopped

4 1/2 oz/125 g smoked salmon

7 oz/200 g large cooked shrimp, thawed if frozen

1 tbsp Dijon mustard

2 tsp superfine sugar

2 tsp red wine vinegar

2 tbsp medium olive oil

few fresh dill sprigs

pepper

warmed rolls or ciabatta bread, to serve

# Tomato, Artichoke & Bean Salad

**SERVES 4–6**

PREPARATION TIME: 10 MINUTES, PLUS 1 HOUR MARINATING

COOKING TIME: NONE

4 ripe plum tomatoes, cut into wedges
4 oz/115 g baby plum tomatoes, halved
14 oz/400 g canned artichoke hearts, drained
14 oz/400 g canned lima beans, drained and rinsed
2 tbsp corn or peanut oil
4 tbsp Thai sweet chili dipping sauce
juice of 1/2 lime
pepper
fresh crusty bread, to serve

*The hot and sweet flavor of the chili dipping sauce gives this salad an extra kick. It is perfect served with lamb chops.*

**1** Place all the tomatoes in a large bowl. Cut the drained artichoke hearts in half, then add to the bowl of tomatoes. Add the lima beans and gently stir together.

**2** Mix the oil, chili dipping sauce, and lime juice together in a small bowl. Season to taste with pepper and pour over the salad. Toss gently until the salad is coated with the dressing.

**3** Cover and let marinate for 1 hour before serving with crusty bread.

# Tomato, Fennel & Apple Salad

**SERVES 4**

PREPARATION TIME: 15 MINUTES

COOKING TIME: NONE

1 small fennel bulb

2 large beefsteak tomatoes, cut into wedges

1 eating apple, quartered, cored, and sliced

6-inch/15-cm piece cucumber, peeled

4 tbsp olive oil

2 tbsp lemon juice

1/2 tsp Dijon mustard

salt and pepper

fennel fronds, to garnish

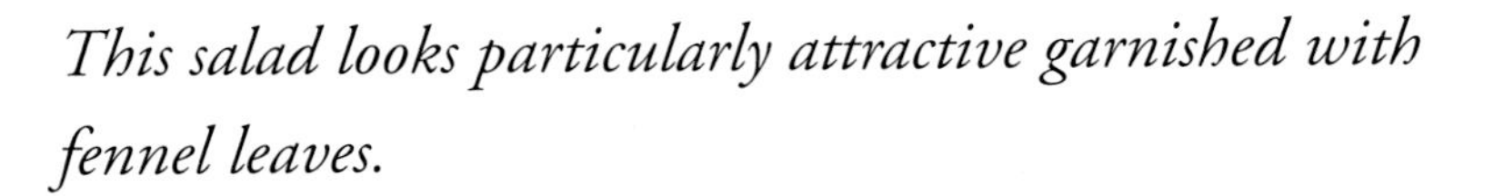

*This salad looks particularly attractive garnished with fennel leaves.*

**1** Using a sharp knife, thinly slice the fennel bulb and place in a large serving dish with the tomato wedges and apple slices.

**2** Cut the cucumber in half lengthwise and, using a teaspoon, scoop out the seeds and discard. Cut each half into thick slices and add to the salad.

**3** Mix the oil, lemon juice, and mustard together in a small bowl. Season to taste with salt and pepper and pour over the salad. Toss gently until the salad is coated with the dressing. Snip the fennel fronds over the top to garnish and serve.

# Tomato & Pine Nut Salad

**SERVES 4**

PREPARATION TIME: 20 MINUTES

COOKING TIME: 15–20 MINUTES

4 ripe plum tomatoes, coarsely chopped
8 oven-dried tomato halves, sliced (see page 14)
1 1/4 cups arugula leaves
4 tbsp pine nuts
9 oz/250 g provolone cheese, drained
3 tbsp olive oil
1 tbsp lemon juice
salt and pepper
warmed pita bread, to serve

2

3

*The heat of the broiled provolone will wilt the arugula slightly and complement the sweetness of the tomatoes.*

**1** Preheat the broiler to medium. Place all the tomatoes in a large serving dish. Add the arugula leaves and toss together.

**2** Dry-fry the pine nuts in a skillet until lightly browned, then sprinkle over the salad.

**3** Cut the provolone cheese into thick slices, then arrange on a large baking sheet. Place under the hot broiler and cook until browned on both sides. Arrange the cheese over the tomato salad.

**4** Mix the oil and lemon juice together in a small bowl. Season with salt and pepper and pour over the salad. Serve at once with warmed pita bread.

# Tomato & Gruyère Tart

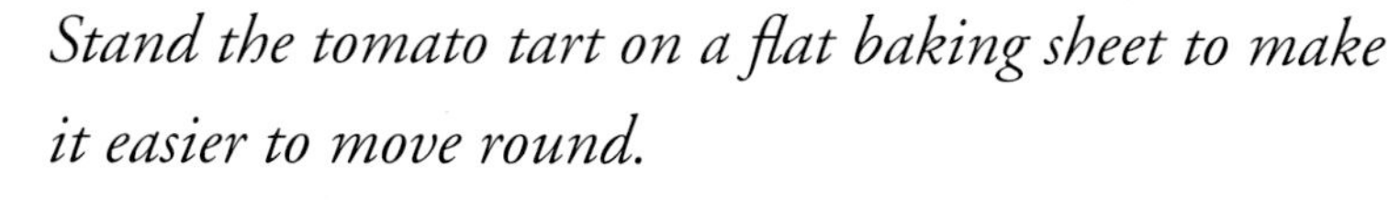
*Stand the tomato tart on a flat baking sheet to make it easier to move round.*

**1** Place the flour in a large bowl. Add the butter and rub it in until the mixture resembles bread crumbs. Add enough water to mix to a firm dough, then roll out on a floured counter and use to line an 8-inch/20-cm tart pan. Prick with a fork and let chill for 1 hour.

**2** Preheat the oven to 400°F/200°C. Heat the oil in a skillet. Add the onions and cook for 10–15 minutes, until browned. Line the base of the pastry shell with foil and bake for 15 minutes, removing the foil after 12 minutes, until lightly browned. Transfer the onions to the pastry shell and sprinkle the cheese on top. Arrange the tomatoes on top of the cheese.

**3** Mix the cream, eggs, and chives together. Season well with salt and pepper and pour into the pastry shell.

**4** Reduce the oven temperature to 350°F/180°C and cook the tart for 30–35 minutes, until set and browned. Garnish with thyme and serve.

**SERVES 6**

PREPARATION TIME: 20 MINUTES, PLUS 1 HOUR CHILLING

COOKING TIME: 1 HOUR–1 HOUR 10 MINUTES

- $1\frac{1}{2}$ cups all-purpose flour, plus extra for dusting
- 4 oz/115 g butter or margarine, cut into small pieces
- 3–4 tbsp water
- 2 tbsp oil
- 2 onions, sliced
- 1 cup Gruyère cheese, grated
- 10 oven-dried tomato halves (see page 14)
- $1\frac{1}{4}$ cups heavy cream
- 2 large eggs
- handful of fresh chives, snipped
- salt and pepper
- few fresh thyme sprigs, to garnish

# Lamb, Tomato & Eggplant Curry

*Choose a curry paste that suits your palate—as hot as you dare.*

**SERVES 4**

PREPARATION TIME: 30 MINUTES

COOKING TIME: 1 HOUR–1 HOUR 10 MINUTES

2 tbsp oil

1 lb 2 oz/500 g lamb fillet or leg, cut into cubes

1 large onion, coarsely chopped

2–3 tbsp curry paste

1 eggplant, cut into small cubes

10 tomatoes, peeled, seeded, and coarsely chopped (see page 6)

$1\frac{3}{4}$ cups canned coconut milk

$1\frac{1}{4}$ cups lamb stock

2 tbsp chopped fresh cilantro

**To serve**

freshly cooked rice

plain yogurt

mango chutney

**1** Heat the oil in a large skillet. Add the lamb in 2–3 batches and cook for 8–10 minutes, or until browned all over. Remove with a slotted spoon and set aside.

**2** Add the onion to the skillet and cook for 2–3 minutes, or until just softened. Add the curry paste and stir-fry for an additional 2 minutes. Add the eggplant, three-quarters of the tomatoes, and the lamb and stir together.

**3** Add the coconut milk and stock and let simmer gently for 30–40 minutes, until the lamb is tender and the curry has thickened.

**4** Mix the remaining tomatoes and cilantro together in a small bowl, then stir into the curry. Serve at once with freshly cooked rice, plain yogurt, and mango chutney.

# Stuffed Tomatoes

**SERVES 4**

PREPARATION TIME: 25 MINUTES

COOKING TIME: 20 MINUTES

4 large, ripe beefsteak tomatoes

1 tbsp oil

8 scallions, chopped

1 red bell pepper, seeded and cut into short strips

2 tbsp chopped fresh parsley

4 oz/115 g fresh bread

$4\frac{1}{2}$ oz/125 g sharp Cheddar cheese

salt and pepper

bay leaves, to garnish

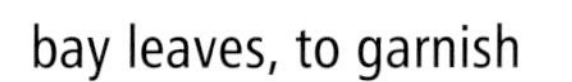

*Choose really ripe and red tomatoes for extra taste and sweetness.*

**1** Preheat the oven to 400°F/200°C. Cut the tops off the tomatoes and, using a sharp knife and teaspoon, scoop out all the seeds. Discard any hard centers, then coarsely chop the remaining flesh and place in a large bowl. Set the tomato shells aside until required.

**2** Heat the oil in a large skillet. Add the scallions and bell pepper and cook for 3–4 minutes, until softened. Add to the tomatoes in the bowl. Place the parsley, bread, and cheese in a food processor and process until finely chopped. Add to the tomato mixture and season well with salt and pepper.

**3** Arrange the tomato shells in a roasting pan. Divide the stuffing between the shells. Cook for 12–15 minutes, or until the tomatoes have softened and collapsed and the stuffing has browned. Garnish with bay leaves and serve at once.

# Baked Cheese & Tomato Soufflés

**SERVES 6**

PREPARATION TIME: 20 MINUTES, PLUS 30–45 MINUTES DRAINING

COOKING TIME: 45–50 MINUTES

6 medium tomatoes, peeled, seeded, and chopped (see page 6)

1 tbsp sugar

2 oz/55 g butter, plus extra for greasing

3/8 cup all-purpose flour

1 1/4 cups milk

4 large eggs, separated

2 cups sharp Cheddar cheese, grated

2 tbsp fresh thyme leaves, plus extra to garnish

*The tomatoes need to drain or they will be too wet for the soufflé to rise properly. Serve with salad greens for a delicious meal.*

**1** Place the tomatoes in a strainer set over a bowl. Sprinkle with the sugar and let drain for 30–45 minutes. Preheat the oven to 350°F/180°C.

**2** Grease and baseline 6 x 1-cup ramekins. Melt the butter in a pan and add the flour. Gradually add the milk, stirring. Bring slowly to a boil, stirring, then let simmer for 2–3 minutes, until thickened. Quickly stir in the egg yolks and remove from the heat. Stir in the cheese and 1 tbsp of the thyme.

**3** Whisk the egg whites in a clean bowl until stiff, then fold into the cheese mixture. Mix the tomatoes and the remaining 1 tbsp of thyme together and divide between the ramekins. Fill each ramekin with the soufflé mixture and stand them in a roasting pan.

**4** Half-fill the roasting pan with hot water and cook for 25–30 minutes, until firm and browned. Turn the soufflés out upside down, garnish with fresh thyme, and serve.

# Salmon Fillet with Concassé Tomatoes

**SERVES 4**

PREPARATION TIME: 30 MINUTES

COOKING TIME: 30–35 MINUTES

4 salmon fillets, about 6 oz/175 g each, trimmed

1 tbsp olive oil

pepper

4 oz/115 g butter

2 bunches asparagus spears, trimmed

6 tomatoes, peeled, seeded, and chopped (see page 6)

1 tbsp chopped fresh dill

grated rind of 1 lemon

*The soft tomatoes make a perfect sauce ingredient to keep the fish moist.*

**1** Preheat the oven to 375°F/190°C. Place the fillets on a cutting board and drizzle with a little oil. Season to taste with pepper. Heat a skillet and cook the fish, nonskin-side down first, until browned. Turn over to brown the other side. Transfer the fish to a roasting pan and cook in the oven for 10–12 minutes, until the fish flakes easily.

**2** Melt the butter in a small pan, then let stand until separated. Pour off the clear, clarified butter into a separate pan, and discard the white salty residue.

**3** Cook the asparagus for 2–3 minutes in boiling water. Drain, rinse under cold running water, drain again, and set aside.

**4** Add the tomatoes, dill, and lemon rind to the butter and heat gently. Divide the asparagus and salmon between 4 plates, spoon some of the tomato dressing over each one, and serve.

# Tomato & Pepperoni Pizza

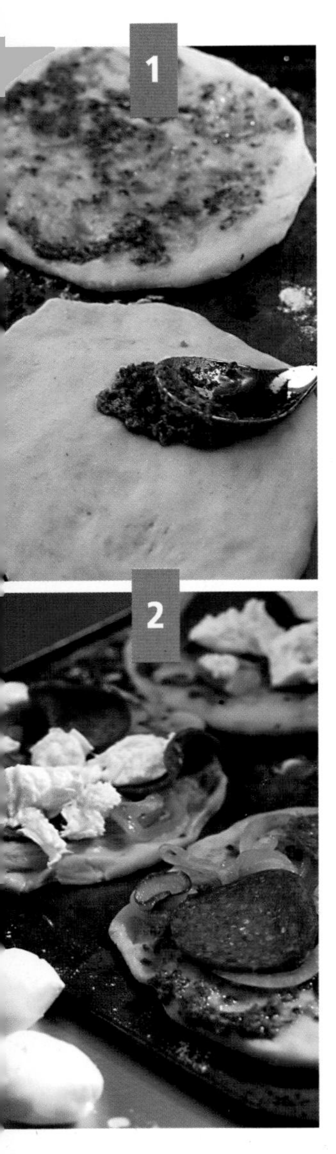


*Cut the dough into four equal pieces to make pizzas for smaller appetites.*

**1** Make up the dough according to the package instructions and once risen flatten out into 4 rough circles. Lift them onto a baking sheet, lightly cover with plastic wrap, and let rise for 20–30 minutes. Spread the pizza bases with pesto.

**2** Preheat the oven to 400°F/200°C. Heat the oil in a large skillet. Add the onions and cook for 3–4 minutes, until softened. Sprinkle over the pizza bases. Arrange the pepperoni and mozzarella cheese slices on top, then tuck in the cherry tomato halves.

**3** Sprinkle the olives and basil over the top. Season well with pepper. Cook the pizzas on a large, lightly oiled baking sheet in the oven for 15–20 minutes, or until the cheese has browned and melted and the bases have risen. Serve at once with salad.

**MAKES 4 X 6-INCH/ 15-CM PIZZAS**

PREPARATION TIME: 30 MINUTES, PLUS 20–30 MINUTES RISING

COOKING TIME: 20–25 MINUTES

1 lb 2 oz/500 g package ready-to-make pizza dough

2 tbsp green pesto

1 tbsp olive oil

2 onions, sliced

2 oz/55 g pepperoni slices

5½ oz/150 g fresh mozzarella cheese, drained and torn

8 oz/225 g cherry tomatoes, halved

12 olives

few fresh basil leaves

pepper

mixed salad, to serve

# Quick Seafood Rice

*Make sure you discard any mussels that don't open or are damaged.*

**1** Heat the oil in a preheated wok or large skillet. Add the onion and cook until just softened. Add the garlic and half the tomatoes and stir together well. Add the rice and stir-fry for 2–3 minutes before adding half the stock and bringing to a boil. Let simmer for 12–15 minutes, adding more stock as necessary.

**2** Add the seafood mixture, mussels, and petit pois. Season to taste with salt and pepper and cook for an additional 3–4 minutes, until hot, the mussels have opened and the liquid has been mostly absorbed. Discard any mussels that remain closed.

**3** Stir in the remaining tomatoes and parsley, taste and adjust the seasoning if necessary, and serve at once with crusty bread.

**SERVES 4**

PREPARATION TIME: 15 MINUTES

COOKING TIME: 25–30 MINUTES

2 tbsp oil
1 large onion, chopped
1 garlic clove, finely chopped
8 large tomatoes, peeled, seeded, and chopped (see page 6)
generous 1 cup paella or risotto rice
3 1/2 cups fish stock
14 oz/400 g mixed seafood mixture, thawed
1 lb/450 g fresh mussels, cleaned
1 1/2 cups petit pois, cooked
salt and pepper
2 tbsp chopped fresh parsley
fresh crusty bread, to serve

# Tomato Rice

**SERVES 4**

PREPARATION TIME: 15 MINUTES

COOKING TIME: 15–20 MINUTES

6 tomatoes
1 tbsp oil
1 large onion, finely chopped
1 tbsp curry paste
1 tsp ground coriander
1 tsp ground cumin
salt and pepper
scant 1 cup basmati rice
2 1/2 cups chicken or vegetable stock
2 tbsp chopped fresh cilantro
8 pappadams, to serve

*The cooked tomatoes add flavor to the rice while the fresh ones add color. Serve with pappadams for a taste of India.*

**1** Cut 4 of the tomatoes in half and cut out the cores, then set aside. Coarsely chop the remaining tomatoes and set aside until required.

**2** Heat the oil in a large pan. Add the onion and cook until softened. Add the reserved tomato halves, curry paste, ground coriander, cumin, and salt and pepper to taste, and cook for 2–3 minutes.

**3** Add the rice and stir-fry for 2–3 minutes. Add the stock and let simmer for 10–12 minutes, or until the rice is tender and the tomatoes have pulped into the mixture. Remove the tomato skins where possible.

**4** Mix the reserved chopped tomatoes and cilantro together in a bowl and stir into the rice mixture. Serve at once with pappadams.

# Tomato & Rosemary Focaccia

**SERVES 8**

PREPARATION TIME: 20 MINUTES, PLUS 1 HOUR 30 MINUTES RISING

COOKING TIME: 15–20 MINUTES

1 lb 2 oz/500 g package rosemary focaccia bread mix

12 oven-dried tomato halves (see page 14)

4 tbsp olive oil

few fresh rosemary sprigs

*The oven-dried tomatoes and rosemary make this a colorful bread to share with friends.*

**1** Place the dry dough mix in a bowl. Coarsely chop half the tomato halves, discarding any skins, and stir into the dough mix. Add enough water to make up the focaccia bread according to the package instructions. Place the prepared dough in an 8-inch/20-cm springform pan.

**2** Preheat the oven to 425°F/220°C. Cut the remaining tomato halves in half. Press your finger into the dough to make indentations and press the tomato quarters into some of them.

**3** Drizzle 3 tbsp of the oil and sprinkle the rosemary sprigs over the top. Let stand for 10 minutes to rise, then cook the focaccia in the oven for 15–20 minutes, or until risen and golden brown. Let cool slightly and drizzle with the remaining oil before serving warm.

# Roasted Tomatoes with Vegetables

*A colorful and tasty accompaniment that adds extra flavor to the simplest of meals, such as pork or lamb chops.*

**1** Preheat the oven to 400°F/200°C. Place all the plum tomatoes and vegetables on a large baking sheet and drizzle with oil.

**2** Arrange the herbs on top, reserving one sprig of thyme for a garnish, and cook in the oven for 20–30 minutes. Toss the vegetables halfway through to coat with the oil. Season to taste with rock salt and pepper and cook for an additional 15–20 minutes, until the vegetables are tender and browned.

**3** Remove the baking sheet from the oven, stir in the chopped tomatoes, garnish with the remaining thyme, and serve at once.

**SERVES 6**

PREPARATION TIME: 30 MINUTES

COOKING TIME: 35–50 MINUTES

6 plum tomatoes, halved
1 red onion, cut into wedges
1 onion, cut into wedges
2 small zucchini, cut into chunks
1 eggplant, cut into chunks
1 red bell pepper, seeded and thickly sliced
5 tbsp olive oil
few fresh rosemary sprigs
few fresh thyme sprigs
1 tbsp rock salt
pepper
2 large tomatoes, coarsely chopped

# Tomato & Potato Tortilla

**SERVES 6**

PREPARATION TIME: 15 MINUTES

COOKING TIME: 30–40 MINUTES

2 lb 4 oz/1 kg potatoes, peeled and cut into small cubes

2 tbsp olive oil

1 bunch of scallions, chopped

4 oz/115 g cherry tomatoes

6 eggs

3 tbsp water

salt and pepper

2 tbsp chopped fresh parsley

*Almost a meal in one, serve this tortilla with salad for lunch or with meat as a main course.*

**1** Cook the potatoes in a pan of lightly salted boiling water for 8–10 minutes, or until tender. Drain and set aside until required.

**2** Preheat the broiler to medium. Heat the oil in a large skillet. Add the scallions and cook until just softened. Add the potatoes and cook for 3–4 minutes, until coated with oil and hot. Smooth the top and sprinkle the tomatoes throughout.

**3** Mix the eggs, water, salt and pepper, and parsley together in a bowl, then pour into the skillet. Cook over very gentle heat for 10–15 minutes, until the tortilla looks fairly set.

**4** Place the skillet under the hot broiler and cook until the top is brown and set. Let cool for 10–15 minutes before sliding out of the skillet onto a cutting board. Cut into wedges and serve at once.

# Index